Across The Midlands

Edited By Katie Douglas

First published in Great Britain in 2017 by:

Young Writers
Remus House
Coltsfoot Drive
Peterborough
PE2 9BF
Telephone: 01733 890066
Website: www.youngwriters.co.uk

All Rights Reserved
Book Design by Spencer Hart
© Copyright Contributors 2017
SB ISBN 978-1-78820-407-1
Printed and bound in the UK by BookPrintingUK
Website: www.bookprintinguk.com

Foreword

Dear Reader,

Welcome to this book packed full of feathery, furry and scaly friends!

Young Writers' Poetry Safari competition was specifically designed for 5-7 year-olds as a fun introduction to poetry and as a way to think about the world of animals. They could write about pets, exotic animals, dinosaurs and you'll even find a few crazy creatures that have never been seen before! From this starting point, the poems could be as simple or as elaborate as the writer wanted, using imagination and descriptive language.

Given the young age of the entrants, we have tried to include as many poems as possible. Here at Young Writers we believe that seeing their work in print will inspire a love of reading and writing and give these young poets the confidence to develop their skills in the future. Poetry is a wonderful way to introduce young children to the idea of rhyme and rhythm and helps learning and development of communication, language and literacy skills.

These young poets have used their creative writing abilities, sentence structure skills, thoughtful vocabulary and most importantly, their imaginations, to make their poems and the animals within them come alive. I hope you enjoy reading them as much as we have.

Katie Douglas

Contents

Independent Entries

Ishaaq Saleem (7)	1
Safaa Alisha Alam (7)	2
Yusraa Hussain (5)	3

Barnack CE Primary School, Barnack

Barnaby Christie (6)	4
Johnny Tyson Hullock (6)	5
Bea Gregory (6)	6
Ellie Rose Moss (6)	7
Jackson Taylor Clarke (6)	8
Charlie Renno (6)	9
Tom Beard (6)	10
Reece Back (6)	11
Ava Marie Foster (5)	12
William Troughton (5)	13

Berridge Primary School, Hyson Green

Ahmed Jamil (7)	14
Muhammed Hussain (7)	16
Sumeyya Kouser Matloob (7)	17
Ria Khan (7)	18
Faria Ahmad (7)	19
Memoona Arif (7)	20
Simra Khan (7)	21

Eastfield Academy, St Albans

Joel Varghese (6)	22
Vera Jegorova (7)	23
Tye Alexandra Raftrey-Lacey (6)	24
Deivids Rasmanis (7)	25

Oak Hill First School, Lodge Park

Maya Smith (6)	26
Julia Zaborowska (6)	27
Charlie Martin (6)	28
Karina Jussab (5)	29
Finlay Page (6)	30
Letrell Joseph (6)	31
Musa Hussain (6)	32
Dawid Braczkowski (6)	33
Mylie Linda Watkinson (6)	34
Harrison Carnall (6)	35
Charlie Russell Meaking (6)	36
Divinna Appiah-Kubi (6)	37
Fearne Ava Milne (6)	38
Sonia Musial (6)	39
Evangeline Gurden (5)	40
Oscar Ball (5)	41
Ashleigh Jane Forman (6)	42
Kingsley Wynter (6)	43
Aaliyah Florence Sienna Ajmal (6)	44
Neve Sharpe (6)	45
Grace Olivia Dawson (5)	46

Our Lady Of Mount Carmel Catholic First School, Webheath

Bailey Lawlor (6)	47
Kalel Read (7)	48
Oliver James Rooke (6)	49
Alfie Twilton (7)	50
Maria Aleksandra Sobala (7)	51
Andrew Owen Molamphy (7)	52
Maja Soloma (7)	53
Lola Antonia Spooner (7)	54

George Doughty (7)	55
Matty Ray Catton (6)	56
Alex Dragun (7)	57
Caitlin McDonnell (7)	58
Oliver James Taaffe (6)	59
Anna Henry-Webb (7)	60
Alyssia Rumbold (7)	61
Olivia Alice Rose (6)	62
Tiana Lei Lawless (7)	63
Jack Lane (7)	64
Hazel Crompton (7)	65
Imogen Lennox (7)	66
Thomas Kieff (7)	67
Lillie-Bett Kate Smith (7)	68
Charlie Michael Haycock (7)	69
Jasmine Ivy Johnson (7)	70
Elliott Joseph Monaghan (7)	71
Elizabeth Mudge (6)	72
Harry Wilson (7)	73
Zack James Martin (7)	74
Lucas Taylor (7)	75
Harriet Louise Kieff (7)	76
Sonia Lipaiova (6)	77
Oliver Matthew Holder (7)	78
Logan Michael Millard (7)	79
Lyla Hadley (7)	80
Noah Hanrahan (7)	81
Shae O'Connor (7)	82
Zofia Siwek (7)	83
Matus Seman (6)	84
Isabella Shaw (7)	85
Mikey O'Connor (7)	86
Oliwia Goska (7)	87

Ranskill Primary School, Ranskill

Robyn Watson (7)	88
Abigail Sofia Tasker (6)	89
Faith Wright (7)	90
Brooklynne Fletcher (7)	91
Abigail Eleanor Veitch (7)	92
Isaac Griffiths (7)	93
Peter Kirsopp (7)	94
Spencer Leon Gee (7)	95

Isaac Frederick Tasker (6)	96
Elise Massam (7)	97
Isabella Jane (7)	98

Somerby Primary School, Somerby

Ellie Barnett (6)	99
Isla Needham (6)	100
Ruby Mann (7)	101
Lucy Wilcox (7)	102

St Edward's Catholic Academy, Swadlincote

Melody-Mae Flanagan-Nicholls (6)	103
Austin Henry Brown (6)	104
Keari Niamh Dickinson (5)	105
Florence Mary Middleton (6)	106
Michal Kusiak (6)	107
Christian Bellafronte (6)	108
Alex Willars (5)	109
Fenella Begley (5)	110
Leni Rae Mercer (6)	111
Illianna Aimee Walters (5)	112
Callum Howard (6)	113
Adam Salter (6)	114
Chaise Leyton Robinson (6)	115
Dylan Kelly (6)	116

St John's CE Primary School & Nursery School, Swindon

Edith Sermon (7)	117
Lexi Hannah Yates (7)	118
Eden Poppy Owen (6)	119
Isabelle Beaman (7)	120
Havana Griffiths (6)	121
Georgia Rose Salter (6)	122

Willington Primary School, Willington

Dhian Singh Sandhu (6)	123

Paige Randle (6)	124
Lola Phillips (6)	125
Olivia Stilwell (6)	126
Jack Chronnell (6)	127
Mia Isabelle Fennell (6)	128
Lacey Harrison (6)	129
Hashim Ahmed (5)	130
Harry Cooke (6)	131
Eli Jacob Cooling (6)	132
Jacob Bull (6)	133
Alba Grace Seals (6)	134
Vivienne Gough (6)	135
Lily Banks (6)	136
Leon Zac Bryan (5)	137
Daisy Broadhurst (6)	138
Maxwell Gene Arnold (6)	139
Lewis Richard Record (6)	140
Harley Neal (6)	141
Ava Marsden (5)	142
Toby Sharp (6)	143
Sienna Sahota (5)	144
Eliza Bethany Scott (6)	145
Jayden Thomas (5)	146

Worlaby Academy, Worlaby

Ryan Hailstone (7)	147
Taya Louise Williams (7)	148
Rosie Harriss (6)	149
Tilly Rose Scott (7)	150
Joey Roberts (6)	151
Ellie Hibbert (6)	152
Freya Allen (6)	153
William George Fowler (6)	154
Alexandra Jorja Carter (6)	155
Lauren-Ava Brunyee (6)	156
Edie Oliver (6)	157
Sophie Gravett (6)	158
Owen Phillips (6)	159
Theo Fletcher (5)	160

Kanarkdra

The kanarkdra is my pet
and he is very funny,
because even though he is an animal,
he cooks pancakes.
Whilst he's cooking,
he jumps up and down excitedly.

Whenever he's eating pancakes
he often snaps his teeth hungrily.
The kanarkdra's favourite food is octopus
because of its sweetness.
He can fly around with his enormous
and tremendous wings.

The kanarkdra is an awesome creature!
Wait till you see him!

Ishaaq Saleem (7)

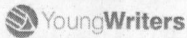

Ruby The Polar Bear

In the icy water of the North Pole,
There lived a polar bear,
She was six years old.
She eats lots of fish,
It is like a big dish,
Her name is Ruby,
She is very spooky.
She loved to swim, and was awfully nice,
But she never swam in the same pool twice!

Safaa Alisha Alam (7)

Tigers

Tigers are orange and black.
They are fast like a train on the track.
Tigers are fluffy and soft.
They have long tails.
They don't eat snails.
They are strong and have big claws.
They are loud and they roar.

Yusraa Hussain (5)

Snake Slither

Snakes look like a very long pencil.
Snakes smell like mud and the river.
Snakes sound like water
coming out of a tap.
Snakes taste like chewy toffee.
Snakes feel very scaly like a fish.

Barnaby Christie (6)
Barnack CE Primary School, Barnack

Monkey Business!

Monkeys taste like chewy chicken.
Monkeys look like swinging chimpanzees.
Monkeys feel like a piece of fluff.
Monkeys sound like a squeaky mouse.
Monkeys smell like the Amazon jungle.

Johnny Tyson Hullock (6)
Barnack CE Primary School, Barnack

Lion

Lions look like a fierce monster
about to eat you.
Lions smell like freshly cooked meat.
Lions feel as soft as a teddy bear.
Lions are like pork
and toffee mixed together.

Bea Gregory (6)
Barnack CE Primary School, Barnack

Lion Roar

Lions look as vicious as an alligator.
Lions smell like meat
Because they eat meat.
Lions feel as soft as a rabbit.
Lions taste like meat.
Lions sound as scary as a dragon.

Ellie Rose Moss (6)
Barnack CE Primary School, Barnack

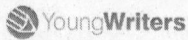

Pigs Like Mud

Pigs smell like chocolate.
Pigs sound like noisy cheetahs.
Pigs taste as yummy as sausages.
Pigs look as beautiful as a butterfly.
Pigs feel as wobbly as jelly.

Jackson Taylor Clarke (6)
Barnack CE Primary School, Barnack

The Aquarium

Fish look like orange swimmers.
They sound like *blob*.
They feel scaly.
They taste like rotten nuts.
They smell like flowers.

Charlie Renno (6)
Barnack CE Primary School, Barnack

Snake Slither

It looks like slime.
It tastes like goo.
It feels like a dragon.
The snake is slithery.
It smells like chocolate.

Tom Beard (6)
Barnack CE Primary School, Barnack

Bear

They are just soft and fluffy.
They look as fluffy as a fox.
They smell like meat.
They sound as loud as a tiger.

Reece Back (6)
Barnack CE Primary School, Barnack

Untitled

Cats smell of fish.
Cats taste of meat.
Cats like to chase mice.
Cats like to jump.
Cats like to hiss.

Ava Marie Foster (5)
Barnack CE Primary School, Barnack

Penguin Slide

Penguins are black.
They are white and good.
Penguins come in the water.

William Troughton (5)
Barnack CE Primary School, Barnack

Dragonfly, Oh Dragonfly

Dragonfly, oh dragonfly
What do you hear?
I hear someone talking about me.
Dragonfly, oh dragonfly
What do you mean?
I mean someone telling his friends about me.
Dragonfly, oh dragonfly
I know what you mean.
You mean someone talking about you.
Dragonfly, oh dragonfly
Where are you?
I'm at the farm visiting a cow that goes moo.
Dragonfly, oh dragonfly
What do you smell?
I smell some candy which is so, so sweet.
Dragonfly, oh dragonfly

Where are you heading?
I'm heading to Africa. Bye-bye.

Ahmed Jamil (7)
Berridge Primary School, Hyson Green

My Friend Elephant

S weet, cute animals named Elephant
A long trunk on its face that is elegant
F at and chubby with a big tummy
A nd all the food it eats is yummy
R ight now its tusks are the best feature
I n the world, there's nothing like this fascinating creature.

Muhammed Hussain (7)
Berridge Primary School, Hyson Green

Monkey

Yes I am a monkey,

M y favourite food is banana,
O nly I am a bit brown,
N one can boss my banana's peel
K ey oo oo aa is what I say
E veryone knows where I live. I love in a zoo
Y es! I am a monkey, not a donkey.

Sumeyya Kouser Matloob (7)
Berridge Primary School, Hyson Green

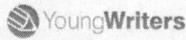

Guess What I Am?

Slippery, rubber skin,
I come in different colours and sizes.
I come from a place that is far and wide,
I have a very long tail,
I've got eyes that look like diamonds
And be careful, because I sting!
What am I?
Can you guess?

Ria Khan (7)
Berridge Primary School, Hyson Green

All About Animals

The animal is really fast.
It is a big cat.
Go and find it running.
Everybody can't catch it.
Run as fast as you can
But you'll never catch it
Until it's tired like a cheetah
And a lion.

Faria Ahmad (7)
Berridge Primary School, Hyson Green

Ants At A Party

Ants on my apple.
Ants on my pear.
Ants crawling everywhere.
Ants on my cake
Making me shake.
Ants are not so great!
How long do I wait till they escape?

Memoona Arif (7)
Berridge Primary School, Hyson Green

A Running Riddle

I live on the African savannah.
I'm yellow and fluffy
But very hard to catch.
I eat animals.
I also fight with lions.
What am I?
A cheetah.

Simra Khan (7)
Berridge Primary School, Hyson Green

Jumbo The Rabbit

I am a jumbo little bunny,
There is nothing so sweet like me.
I am so cuddly, not scary.
Children like to pat, pat, pat me.
My soft little ear goes *flop, flop, flop.*
My silky tail goes *flip, flip, flip.*
My cheeky little nose goes *cheek, cheek, cheek.*
I am a jumbo and I am clever.
I have two little blue eyes.

Joel Varghese (6)
Eastfield Academy, St Albans

My Bunny Bella

Bella is my bunny.
I think he is funny.
He eats pizza and plays football
And doesn't like carrots at all.
His fur is soft and grey.
He loves to hop, run and play.
We had him for seven years.
He has big, floppy ears.
He lives in his hutch.
I love him so much.
My Bella is a funny fella.

Vera Jegorova (7)
Eastfield Academy, St Albans

Mister Meerkat

Hello, Mister Meerkat.
Who's a cat?
Me, a cat?
Fancy that...

Do you meow?
Do you howl?
Do you have a terrible growl?

No, no, not me,
I have tall legs, so I can see.
I run fast so you can't catch me.
I am a meerkat,
I'm much better than a cat.

Tye Alexandra Raftrey-Lacey (6)
Eastfield Academy, St Albans

The Parrot

A parrot flying past the trees,
Up in the sky and past the sea,
Finding food and no luck for him,
But finally found his friends and me,
His long tail brushing the branches
And with his pointy beak calling his friends,
Never mind if they don't care
'Cause what kind of parrot is he?

Deivids Rasmanis (7)
Eastfield Academy, St Albans

In The Jungle

In the jungle, in the jungle
Long snake slithering slowly
through the grass.
Slithering, bumpy crocodile
sneaking through the water.
Proud, fierce lion roaring loudly
on the top of the rock.
Stripy, black and white zebra
galloping through the grass.
Swishy, stripy tiger sprinting loudly
through the field.
Huge, grey elephant stomping
through the butterflies.
Tall, yellow giraffe chomping
on the leaves in the trees.
In the jungle.

Maya Smith (6)
Oak Hill First School, Lodge Park

In The Jungle

In the jungle, in the jungle
scary, green snakes slowly
slithering through the grass.
In the jungle, in the jungle
furry, fast lions quickly
running through the trees.
In the jungle, in the jungle
colourful, noisy parrots
angrily flying in the air.
In the jungle, in the jungle
fierce, furry tigers prowling
creepily through the plants.
In the jungle, in the jungle
what do you hear?

Julia Zaborowska (6)
Oak Hill First School, Lodge Park

In The Jungle

In the jungle, in the jungle
stripy zebras quickly running
through the savannah.
In the jungle, in the jungle
bouncy kangaroos cheekily
jumping in the air.
In the jungle, in the jungle
noisy parrots loudly flapping
through the trees.
In the jungle, in the jungle
angry lions scarily prowling
through the grasslands.
In the jungle, in the jungle
what do you hear?

Charlie Martin (6)
Oak Hill First School, Lodge Park

In The Jungle

Fast, spotty cheetah running in the jungle.
Big gorilla swinging on a long tree branch.
A ginormous hippo splashing in the water.
Bumpy crocodile snapping his teeth
up and down.
A long and slimy snake slithering
on the jungle floor.
A stripy tiger is roaring loudly.
A monkey who is brown
and funny to listen to.
An elephant who stamps on wood.

Karina Jussab (5)
Oak Hill First School, Lodge Park

In The Jungle

In the jungle, in the jungle
Soft elephant stomping.
In the jungle, in the jungle
Bumpy crocodile sleeping.
In the jungle, in the jungle
Stripy, smooth zebra jumping.
In the jungle, in the jungle
Frightened tiger chomping.
In the jungle, in the jungle
Greedy snake slithering.
In the jungle, in the jungle
What can you hear?

Finlay Page (6)
Oak Hill First School, Lodge Park

In The Jungle

In the jungle, in the jungle
stripy zebras quickly running
past the waterhole.
In the jungle, in the jungle
furry tigers loudly growling in the bushes.
In the jungle, in the jungle
huge elephants loudly stomping in the river.
In the jungle, in the jungle
Noisy parrots selfishly squawking
early in the morning.
What do you hear?

Letrell Joseph (6)
Oak Hill First School, Lodge Park

In The Jungle

In the jungle, in the jungle
Fierce, bumpy rhino charging.
In the jungle, in the jungle
Giant tiger sleeping.
In the jungle, in the jungle
Stripy snake slithering.
In the jungle, in the jungle
Stripy zebra eating.
In the jungle, in the jungle
Sharp-toothed hippo drinking.
In the jungle, in the jungle.

Musa Hussain (6)
Oak Hill First School, Lodge Park

In The Jungle

In the jungle, in the jungle
Soft bear eating.
In the jungle, in the jungle
Fierce, sharp tiger running.
In the jungle, in the jungle
Long-necked giraffe eating.
In the jungle, in the jungle
Sneaky chimpanzee swinging.
In the jungle, in the jungle
Long snake slithering.
In the jungle, in the jungle.

Dawid Braczkowski (6)
Oak Hill First School, Lodge Park

In The Jungle

In the jungle, in the jungle
Fierce lion roaring.
In the jungle, in the jungle
The cheeky monkeys laugh too much.
In the jungle, in the jungle
Stripy tigers roaring on the rock.
In the jungle, in the jungle
Slithery snakes hissing.
In the jungle, in the jungle
Spotted giraffes chomping.

Mylie Linda Watkinson (6)
Oak Hill First School, Lodge Park

In The Jungle

In the jungle, in the jungle
Fluffy, fast zebras running.
In the jungle, in the jungle
Green, fierce snakes slithering.
In the jungle, in the jungle
Cheeky, hungry monkeys swinging.
In the jungle, in the jungle
Wet, smooth hippos splashing.
In the jungle, in the jungle
What do you hear?

Harrison Carnall (6)
Oak Hill First School, Lodge Park

In The Jungle

In the jungle, in the jungle
Naughty monkeys quickly swinging.
In the jungle, in the jungle
Noisy parrots quickly flying.
In the jungle, in the jungle
Long, green snake slithering.
In the jungle, in the jungle
Soft, vicious lions prowling.
In the jungle, in the jungle
What do you hear?

Charlie Russell Meaking (6)
Oak Hill First School, Lodge Park

In The Jungle

In the jungle, in the jungle
Cheeky chimpanzees swinging.
In the jungle, in the jungle
The fierce lion roaring.
In the jungle, in the jungle
Fast tiger running.
In the jungle, in the jungle
Long snake slithering.
In the jungle, in the jungle
What do you hear?
I hear a tiger.

Divinna Appiah-Kubi (6)
Oak Hill First School, Lodge Park

In The Jungle

In the jungle, in the jungle
Cheeky, naughty monkey swinging.
In the jungle, in the jungle
Soft green parrot flying.
In the jungle, in the jungle
Stripy, fast zebras jumping.
In the jungle, in the jungle
Fierce, funny tiger roaring.
In the jungle, in the jungle
What do you hear?

Fearne Ava Milne (6)
Oak Hill First School, Lodge Park

In The Jungle

In the jungle, in the jungle
Cheeky, noisy monkeys swinging.
In the jungle, in the jungle
Cheeky, fast tigers walking.
In the jungle, in the jungle
Green, fast snakes walking.
In the jungle, in the jungle
Noisy, fast parrot flying.
In the jungle, in the jungle
What do you hear?

Sonia Musial (6)
Oak Hill First School, Lodge Park

In The Jungle

In the jungle, in the jungle
Huge, noisy elephants.
In the jungle, in the jungle
Colourful, grumpy parrot flapping.
In the jungle, in the jungle
Cheeky, furry monkeys.
In the jungle, in the jungle
Green, scaly snakes slithering.
In the jungle, in the jungle
What do you hear?

Evangeline Gurden (5)
Oak Hill First School, Lodge Park

In The Jungle

In the jungle, in the jungle
Fierce, bumpy rhino chewing.
In the jungle, in the jungle
Fierce leopards pouncing.
In the jungle, in the jungle
Cheeky monkeys swinging.
In the jungle, in the jungle
Slithery snakes slithering.

Oscar Ball (5)
Oak Hill First School, Lodge Park

In The Jungle

In the jungle, in the jungle
Tall giraffes running fast.
Long snake slithering slowly.
Cheeky chimpanzee swinging fast.
Huge grey elephant stomping loudly.
Stripy zebra galloping fast.
In the jungle, in the jungle.

Ashleigh Jane Forman (6)
Oak Hill First School, Lodge Park

In The Jungle

In the jungle, in the jungle
Cheeky monkey swinging.

In the jungle, in the jungle
Spotty cheetah running fast.

In the jungle, in the jungle
Elegant, fierce tiger scratching.

Kingsley Wynter (6)
Oak Hill First School, Lodge Park

In The Jungle

In the jungle, in the jungle
Huge, grey elephant stomping loudly.
Long, smooth snake slithering slowly.
Proud lion roaring loudly.
Stripy zebra galloping quickly.
In the jungle, in the jungle.

Aaliyah Florence Sienna Ajmal (6)
Oak Hill First School, Lodge Park

Animals

In the jungle, in the jungle
Big, large hippo stomping loudly.
Scary, terrifying lion sneaking all around.
A large elephant stomping.
Cheetah running very fast.
In the jungle, in the jungle.

Neve Sharpe (6)
Oak Hill First School, Lodge Park

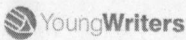

In The Jungle

In the jungle, in the jungle
Hungry grey elephants stomping loudly.
Stripy, white zebras galloping.
Tall, yellow and brown giraffes chewing.
Large, smooth snakes slithering.

Grace Olivia Dawson (5)
Oak Hill First School, Lodge Park

Cool Crazy Croc

Cool Croc was all scaly and green,
He was so friendly and never ever mean.
His favourite food was chocolate bars,
Mainly Maltesers, Snickers and Mars.
He was scaly, green and had a podgy belly
As he liked to sit down and watch telly.
He also liked working in his music shop,
He could always find time to do a jig and bop.
He lived high in a flat overlooking the city
And lived with his dog, his mouse and his kitty.
Cool Croc was the craziest croc you'll ever meet,
As he even wore sunglasses upon his feet.

Bailey Lawlor (6)
Our Lady Of Mount Carmel Catholic First School, Webheath

My Pet Auto-Crasher

My pet, Auto-Crasher, is faster than Dasher,
Because he has magical powers.
He has six legs and six spiky heads
Which means he can bark really loud.
He lives in a cave
Because he is brave,
So I visit him once a year.
We have a talk and a little walk,
Then after I tickle his ear.
He likes to eat lava
Because it makes him fly.
He can travel across the sky.
When I go home I feel very sad and
I miss him when I say goodbye.

Kalel Read (7)
Our Lady Of Mount Carmel Catholic First School, Webheath

My Pet Fudge

Fudge has been my cat since
I can remember,
He used to wake me every morning
By jumping on my bed.
He liked to sit upon my lap
For lots of love and cuddles.
Fudge always purrs when happy.
Fudge was 12 years old
And has led a wonderful life.
Today I said goodbye to Fudge.
It was very sad.
He has gone to Heaven
And I will remember him
By looking up at the stars every night.
God bless Fudge, my beautiful cat.

Oliver James Rooke (6)
Our Lady Of Mount Carmel Catholic First School, Webheath

Hei Hei

Hei Hei is a chick as crazy as can be,
He's scared of everything,
Especially the deep blue sea.
He's in the film 'Moana',
They crossed the ocean wide.
He wears a coconut on his head
But he's good to be by your side.
He's yellow, green, blue, orange and red.
He must have fallen and hit his head.
His eyes are crossed.
He keeps getting lost and ending up at sea.

Alfie Twilton (7)
Our Lady Of Mount Carmel Catholic First School, Webheath

Butterflies

When I'm looking at the sky
I can see a butterfly.
It is blue, it is pink,
It is as beautiful as spring.
It is small and it can fly,
Please don't touch the butterfly.
If you touch his wing it won't be able to fly
And you will never see a butterfly up in the sky.
Let me tell you one thing,
Butterfly is an insect
But it looks absolutely perfect.

Maria Aleksandra Sobala (7)
Our Lady Of Mount Carmel Catholic First School, Webheath

If I Were A Dolphin

If I were a dolphin, I'd live in the sea,
I'd swim, be warm and feel so happy
To be with my friends, leap into the sky,
What a joy it would be to be flying so high!
Down in the ocean we play lots of games,
But the goldfish,
They struggle to remember our names.
But we all get along, as well as can be,
What a life to be had
When you're under the sea!

Andrew Owen Molamphy (7)
Our Lady Of Mount Carmel Catholic First School, Webheath

My Poppy

I would love my dog very much
And her name would be Poppy.
She would have her nose as black as coal
And her ears would be floppy.
We would be friends till the end
And always full of joy,
Always happy and ready to play,
She would be my friend, not my toy.
I would play with her every day
And do lots of activities
And never forget my responsibilities.

Maja Soloma (7)
Our Lady Of Mount Carmel Catholic First School, Webheath

My Cute Friend, Louie

Louie, I love it when we play
And you run around all day.
Sometimes you nip at my toes
But I can't be mad
When you wiggle your cute little nose.

Louie, I love it when we go for walks,
I'm sorry if I talk, talk, talk too much.
When I see you sleeping in your bed
I know thoughts of me are in your head.

I love you Louie.

Lola Antonia Spooner (7)
Our Lady Of Mount Carmel Catholic First School, Webheath

My Dog Marley

My dog Marley is fluffy and cute.
His nose is brown and he runs around.
He wags his tail to say hello
And jumps up and down like a yo-yo.
He likes to chase the ball around
And is fast on the ground.
A dental stick is his favourite thing
To keep his teeth nice and clean.
I love my dog, he is the best,
A family member he will always be.

George Doughty (7)
Our Lady Of Mount Carmel Catholic First School, Webheath

Cheetahs

C heetahs are medium-sized cats
H ungry for their prey
E very animal has their own habitat
E ating gazelles on their way
T heir teeth are sharp and pointy
A nd their tails are long and thin
H appy when they are free and running
S uper quiet when they're stalking.

Matty Ray Catton (6)
Our Lady Of Mount Carmel Catholic First School, Webheath

Snake Party

In the mountains far away
Where the sun is bright and the clouds are grey,
The snake had a party.
His two best friends were called Marty and Smarty.
The snake wished to have a mouse cake.
The mouse is always a favourite food for a snake.
The mouse was fast and ran away
But his friends made his day great anyway.

Alex Dragun (7)
Our Lady Of Mount Carmel Catholic First School, Webheath

Penguins

    P enguins live in the Antarctic
    E verywhere they go it snows
    N ever will you see a penguin fly
    G o and see a penguin at the Sealife
yo **U** can go and see a penguin slide
    I gloos are where the penguins hide
    N ow go and find more about a penguin's life.

Caitlin McDonnell (7)
Our Lady Of Mount Carmel Catholic First School, Webheath

My Dragon

My dragon is very mean.
He likes to eat people with beans.
My dragon is very scary.
Once he tried to eat a fairy.
My dragon is very bad.
He even tried to eat my dad.
My dragon is not nice.
He likes to eat people with rice.
Watch out, beware, be alert,
My dragon wants some dessert.

Oliver James Taaffe (6)
Our Lady Of Mount Carmel Catholic First School, Webheath

Cotton Our Lovely Cat

I love Cotton and she is our cat,
She gets very happy
When I give her a gentle pat.
Sometimes she can be lazy
And sometimes she can be in a fury.

When Cotton eats a lot
She gets a big, fat tummy.
Cotton is a black and white cat,
Just like Postman Pat's cat.

Anna Henry-Webb (7)
Our Lady Of Mount Carmel Catholic First School, Webheath

My Cat Molly

I have a cat named Molly.
She is nice and fluffy.
She sometimes sleeps on my bed
And sometimes on Mummy's.
She loves a fuss which makes her purr
But I don't like her fur,
It makes me sneeze.
She loves climbing trees to catch birds.
I hope she doesn't get fleas.

Alyssia Rumbold (7)
Our Lady Of Mount Carmel Catholic First School, Webheath

Derek The Donkey

My name is Derek and I am a donkey.
I have four legs but one is wonky.

My eyesight is not very clear
One day I looked in the mirror
And thought I was a deer.

I go out at night to play in the park,
As the carrots I eat
Help me to see in the dark.

Olivia Alice Rose (6)
Our Lady Of Mount Carmel Catholic First School, Webheath

A Dog On A Log

I once saw a dog
Who was sat on a log.
As I walked across a field one day
The field was full of hay
And I shouted, 'Come and play.'
But then he ran away.
As I walked closer
I then saw a frog
That was stuck in a bog
All on a bright summer's day.

Tiana Lei Lawless (7)
Our Lady Of Mount Carmel Catholic First School, Webheath

Baxter The Fluffy Cat

Baxter is my fluffy cat,
His fur is soft as snow.
He has a lovely brown face
And big blue eyes that glow.
He likes to go for walks at night
And sleeps all through the day
But when we come home from school
Baxter the fluffy cat always wants to play.

Jack Lane (7)
Our Lady Of Mount Carmel Catholic First School, Webheath

Koala Adventure

Koalas live a way away.
They sleep most of the day.

They eat leaves from trees
But they don't eat carrots, beans and peas.

They are grey
To keep the sun away,

They are very rare
So you must take care.

Hazel Crompton (7)
Our Lady Of Mount Carmel Catholic First School, Webheath

Spiders Run And Hide

S miley, happy little friend
P olitely saying, 'Sorry Fly for trying to eat you.'
I was very hungry back then.
'D on't eat me bird!'
E ight wiggly, crawly, long legs.
R un very fast to hide.

Imogen Lennox (7)
Our Lady Of Mount Carmel Catholic First School, Webheath

About Fruit Bats

I'm a fruit bat can't you see?
I love flapping my wings from tree to tree.

I love hanging upside down,
The world looks fabulous this side around.

Give me fruit all day long...
And I might just sing you a song.

Thomas Kieff (7)
Our Lady Of Mount Carmel Catholic First School, Webheath

Bobby Bird The Parakeet

Bobby is my pet parakeet,
He really is very sweet.
He sings and tweets all the day.
When I see him I shout, 'Hooray!'
He says, 'Hello', and 'what you doing?'
But put your finger near the cage,
He will be chewing!

Lillie-Bett Kate Smith (7)
Our Lady Of Mount Carmel Catholic First School, Webheath

Crazy Cookie

My cat called Cookie is crazy.
She lies in the sun.
She is a little bit lazy.
She can be very nice
But likes to chase mice.
She's very, very cheeky
And really, really sneaky.
She makes a loud, loud purr,
I absolutely love her.

Charlie Michael Haycock (7)
Our Lady Of Mount Carmel Catholic First School, Webheath

Bunny, Hop, Hop, Hop

Bunnies are cute.
Bunnies are small.
Bunnies hardly eat anything at all
But they are still a big round ball.

Cuddly and furry
But they are wary.
Timid and placid but kind and sweet
And they will not retreat.

Jasmine Ivy Johnson (7)
Our Lady Of Mount Carmel Catholic First School, Webheath

Cheetahs

C hase animals to eat
H ot open grasslands
E scape to run free
E at mammals for tea
T ail like a rudder
A ssisting, running fast
H as spots for camouflage
S urviving all odds.

Elliott Joseph Monaghan (7)
Our Lady Of Mount Carmel Catholic First School, Webheath

The Queen Butterfly

Whirly, twirly, flutter and fly
Round and round the butterfly.

Queeny, Queeny butterfly
Came to me and sung a lullaby.

Sleepy, sleepy, I'm in a dream,
Thank you, thank you, oh my queen.

Elizabeth Mudge (6)
Our Lady Of Mount Carmel Catholic First School, Webheath

A Beautiful Butterfly

A beautiful butterfly fluttering around,
It doesn't make a sound.
A beautiful butterfly
Flying high in the bright blue sky.
Its colourful wings glistening in the sun.
The beautiful butterfly is having lots of fun.

Harry Wilson (7)
Our Lady Of Mount Carmel Catholic First School, Webheath

My Pet Dog

My dog is called Bentley,
I stroke him very gently.
He likes to go for a walk,
He cannot talk.
He barks when he sees cats.
I like when he lies across my lap.
I hope he can see
That he is very special to me.

Zack James Martin (7)
Our Lady Of Mount Carmel Catholic First School, Webheath

Milo The Rhino

There once was a rhino called Milo
Who liked to swim in the Nilo.
He ate his food by the pilo.
His best friend was a tigo
And they danced on the lino
Only after drinking their wino
Right by the Nilo.

Lucas Taylor (7)
Our Lady Of Mount Carmel Catholic First School, Webheath

Butterflies

Munch, munch, crunch, crunch,
Wiggle, wiggle, giggle, giggle,
Spin, spin around, up and down,
Sleep, sleep, grow, grow,
Sleep some more for a week or two,
Hello, guess what I am?

Harriet Louise Kieff (7)
Our Lady Of Mount Carmel Catholic First School, Webheath

Frog Under The Log

Woke up in the morning to see a fog.
After the breakfast we went for a walk
And there, by a rock was lying a log
And under the log was sitting a frog
My dog saw the frog
And jumped through the log.

Sonia Lipaiova (6)
Our Lady Of Mount Carmel Catholic First School, Webheath

I Miss Scooby

I really miss Scooby.
He always used to play with me.
He always did tricks.
He loved big sticks.
Why do dogs have to die?
Thinking about this makes me cry.
Why can't dogs live forever?

Oliver Matthew Holder (7)
Our Lady Of Mount Carmel Catholic First School, Webheath

My Cat

I have a pet cat
And his name is Chief.
Taking all my toys, what a thief.
Every now and again
He will come out for a peep
But usually he doesn't
Because he's always asleep.

Logan Michael Millard (7)
Our Lady Of Mount Carmel Catholic First School, Webheath

Funny Things About My Dog

I have a crazy dog called Bo.
She likes to run and go!
One day in the park
Not so very far from home
She gave a great big bark
And would not come home
So I went home alone.

Lyla Hadley (7)
Our Lady Of Mount Carmel Catholic First School, Webheath

Mikey The Caterpillar

Mikey the caterpillar
Had eaten a leaf,
He built a cocoon
And fell asleep.

When it was morning
He opened his eyes
And to his surprise
He was a butterfly.

Noah Hanrahan (7)
Our Lady Of Mount Carmel Catholic First School, Webheath

Snake

There was a slippery snake
Who lived near a lake.
He liked to eat ants
But he never wore pants.
He slithered here,
He slithered there,
He slithered everywhere!

Shae O'Connor (7)
Our Lady Of Mount Carmel Catholic First School, Webheath

A Fat Cat

One cat is fat,
He chats with a bat
About another skinny cat
Because he's never seen a plate
And he wants to eat a rat
Because he doesn't want to be flat.

Zofia Siwek (7)
Our Lady Of Mount Carmel Catholic First School, Webheath

Spider

Spider is a great wall rider.
No fly is safe.
No fly dares
When Spider is there.
He is like a big bear.
When flies don't care
Food is there.

Matus Seman (6)
Our Lady Of Mount Carmel Catholic First School, Webheath

My Cat, Princess

I have a cat called Princess.
We think she's a bit fat
But she couldn't care less
Because she looks good in a dress.
That's my cat, Princess.

Isabella Shaw (7)
Our Lady Of Mount Carmel Catholic First School, Webheath

Brown Bear

Brown Bear loves to scare.
He does not share.
Nobody cares for the bear.
He says a prayer.
He eats pears.
He likes to breathe the air.

Mikey O'Connor (7)
Our Lady Of Mount Carmel Catholic First School, Webheath

Trusio Trusio

Trusio Trusio, he is a bunny.
Trusio Trusio, he is funny.
Trusio Trusio quickly running
And the most he likes high jumping.

Oliwia Goska (7)
Our Lady Of Mount Carmel Catholic First School, Webheath

Horse

Brown horse, quick and small,
He's the same colour as the bumpy wall.

Pretty horse, white and black,
Spends all his life carrying a sack.

Naughty horse, very quick,
Sometimes he even does a kick.

Lucky horse, in the muck,
His shoes are supposed to be so much luck.

Robyn Watson (7)
Ranskill Primary School, Ranskill

Cat And Dog

Happy cat, short and small
Wherever he is he is climbing the wall.

Short cat, black and white
Who is always ready for a fight.

Little dog, short and hairy
When he is ready for messing up the dairy.

Abigail Sofia Tasker (6)
Ranskill Primary School, Ranskill

Farm Animals

Little horse, furry and brown
Who lives on a farm in a town.

A cow, all hairy and black
Who sometimes wears a little hat.

Small pig, all fluffy and pink
Who always does a little wink.

Faith Wright (7)
Ranskill Primary School, Ranskill

Pets

Little dog fluffy and brown
Lives in a smelly town.

A little cat is ginger and white,
His body is very light.

A little horse is tall and black
Eating from a sack.

Brooklynne Fletcher (7)
Ranskill Primary School, Ranskill

Dog

A shadow-barker.
A curtain-biter.
A fast-runner.
A sensible-walker.
A quick-eater.
A silly-bumper.
A toy-chewer.
A person-nibbler.
A lazy-sleeper.
A bone-cruncher.

Abigail Eleanor Veitch (7)
Ranskill Primary School, Ranskill

Animals

Brown horse so brown,
He lives in a town.
Little pig in the mud,
Having a roll after the flood.
Little cat so cheeky and small,
No wonder I see him on every wall.

Isaac Griffiths (7)
Ranskill Primary School, Ranskill

Mouse

A stealthy walker.
A sneaky eater.
A fast walker.
A quick digger.
A box chewer.
A cheese eater.
A loud squeaker.
A cat escaper.

Peter Kirsopp (7)
Ranskill Primary School, Ranskill

Pig

A loud snorer.
A sloppy mud bather.
A fast meat eater.
A loud oinker.
A peaceful sunbather.
A slow stretcher.

Spencer Leon Gee (7)
Ranskill Primary School, Ranskill

Pets

Little dog fluffy and hairy
Chasing cows in the dairy.
Little goldfish smooth and wet,
You make a very good pet.

Isaac Frederick Tasker (6)
Ranskill Primary School, Ranskill

Pig

A loud snorter.
A chompy eater.
A slurpy eater.
A loud sleeper.
A fast walker.
A slop lover.

Elise Massam (7)
Ranskill Primary School, Ranskill

Dog

A fast runner.
A messy eater.
A noisy barker.
A bed chewer.
A dog fighter.
A shed climber.

Isabella Jane (7)
Ranskill Primary School, Ranskill

Jumping Snow Leopard

L eopards' spots tell a story
E ating hares and sheep for his tea
O ne magnificent, long sleek tail wraps around him
P eople spot the snow leopard but keep away
A lone at the top of the mountain
R eady to pounce!
D aylight shines on his beautiful spotty coat
S now hides him safe and sound.

Ellie Barnett (6)
Somerby Primary School, Somerby

Minion Cat

Minion Cat sits on a mat
Eating his favourite food,
Eat your tuna and your fish
Then he has to clean the dish and spoon.
Very tired, bored and hot
Then he decides he needs a rest.
Minion Cat, what do you see?
Minion Cat needs a sleep.

Isla Needham (6)
Somerby Primary School, Somerby

Abigail's Horse

Abigail, Abigail on her horse.
Abigail racing around the course.
Jumping and trotting over the fence.
The crowd all watch, feeling really tense.
Abigail's horse canters very fast.
He races and races and never comes last.

Ruby Mann (7)
Somerby Primary School, Somerby

The King Lion

The lion is loud
And he walks around
Being mighty and proud.
He is very hairy and scary
With a big roar he uses his claws
To pierce his dinner.
He is very fierce.

Lucy Wilcox (7)
Somerby Primary School, Somerby

Penguin

Penguin,
Black, icy-white,
Spooky eyes, black beak, black wings,
Bellyflop, swimming, waddle, squeak,
Ugly feet, white and black skin, orange skin,
Cute, adorable,
Penguin.

Melody-Mae Flanagan-Nicholls (6)
St Edward's Catholic Academy, Swadlincote

Dinosaur

Dinosaurs,
Fast, powerful,
Spine, jaw, beak,
Fighting, munching, dashing, gliding,
Nostrils, eyes, nails,
Mighty, enormous,
Dinosaurs.

Austin Henry Brown (6)
St Edward's Catholic Academy, Swadlincote

Penguin

Penguin,
Cute, fluffy,
Eyes, beak, feet,
Bellyflop, waddle, flapping, swimming,
Flippers, wings, fur,
Jet-black, icy-white,
Penguin.

Keari Niamh Dickinson (5)
St Edward's Catholic Academy, Swadlincote

Dinosaurs

Dinosaurs,
Scary, large,
Horns, spines, spikes,
Stretching, flying, walking, hunting,
Neck, tail, wings,
Nice, large,
Dinosaurs.

Florence Mary Middleton (6)
St Edward's Catholic Academy, Swadlincote

Penguin

Penguin,
Black, soft,
Eyes, feet, fur,
Running, bellyflop, swimming, pouncing,
Beak, claws, flippers,
White, fluffy,
Penguin.

Michal Kusiak (6)
St Edward's Catholic Academy, Swadlincote

Tiger

Tiger,
Petite, sharp,
Eyes, beak, feet,
Roaring, running, whooshing, swimming,
Claws, paws, whiskers,
Massive, strong,
Tiger.

Christian Bellafronte (6)
St Edward's Catholic Academy, Swadlincote

Dinosaurs

Dinosaurs,
Scary, spiky,
Horns, teeth, neck,
Running, flying, creeping, hunting,
Claws, feet, fins,
Fast, strong,
Dinosaurs.

Alex Willars (5)
St Edward's Catholic Academy, Swadlincote

Tiger

Tiger,
Wet, black,
Teeth, claws, paws,
Falling, running, pouncing, purring,
Eyes, whiskers, teeth,
Orange, stripes,
Tiger.

Fenella Begley (5)
St Edward's Catholic Academy, Swadlincote

Penguin

Penguin,
Soft, fluffy,
Beak, feet, eyes,
Waddling, diving, swimming, feeding,
Wings, flippers, fur,
White, heavy,
Penguin.

Leni Rae Mercer (6)
St Edward's Catholic Academy, Swadlincote

Tiger

Tiger,
Orange, fast,
Teeth, claws, feet,
Roaring, running, snarling, flapping,
Tail, paws, black,
Massive whiskers,
Tiger.

Illianna Aimee Walters (5)
St Edward's Catholic Academy, Swadlincote

Tiger

Tiger,
Strong, soft,
Eyes, fur, paws,
Running, pouncing, roaring, snarling,
Whiskers, stripes, tail,
Black, white
Tiger.

Callum Howard (6)
St Edward's Catholic Academy, Swadlincote

Tiger

Tiger,
Petite, orange,
Fur, feet, eyes,
Swimming, running, roaring, whooshing,
Claws, teeth, eyes,
Black, white,
Tiger.

Adam Salter (6)
St Edward's Catholic Academy, Swadlincote

Roaring Tiger

Tiger,
Petite, soft,
Eyes, beak, feet,
Running, roaring, diving, snarling,
Flippers, claws, tail,
Claws, huge,
Tiger.

Chaise Leyton Robinson (6)
St Edward's Catholic Academy, Swadlincote

Penguin

Penguin,
Black, grey,
Feet, eyes, fur,
Diving, swimming, bellyflop, waddle,
Claws, beak, tail,
Soft, big,
Penguin.

Dylan Kelly (6)
St Edward's Catholic Academy, Swadlincote

Kind Giraffes

G raceful giraffes look beautiful
I nto the top of the trees they reach
R ipping the leaves with their long black tongue
A frica is their home or zoos around the world
F ighting each other with their horns
F riendly when you meet them
E dith's favourite animal
S pecial and unique.

Edith Sermon (7)
St John's CE Primary School & Nursery School, Swindon

Stripy Tiger

S is for scary
T is for teeth
R is for roar
I is for immaculate coat
P is for predator
Y is for yawning in the daytime.

T is for terrifying
I is for intelligent
G is for greedy
E is for enormous
R is for really good swimmer.

Lexi Hannah Yates (7)
St John's CE Primary School & Nursery School, Swindon

The Singing And Dancing Gorilla

One sunny morning all was still.
The gorilla was asleep on a hill.
He was woken up by his favourite song
And he jumped out of bed like King Kong.
He grabbed a banana and sang in it.
He did a little dance
In just his pants.
He put the banana down,
Then did a wiggle with his bum
All the way round.

Eden Poppy Owen (6)
St John's CE Primary School & Nursery School, Swindon

Melvin The Magnificent Meerkat

M elvin was his name
E ating was his game
E veryone liked him
R ummaging for food in the bin
K eeping his eye out for thieves stealing his food
A ngry Melvin might get in a mood
T ake it easy Melvin, don't be rude.

Isabelle Beaman (7)
St John's CE Primary School & Nursery School, Swindon

The Zebras And The Lions

As the lions pass,
The zebras hide in the grass.
The lion's roar is loud enough
To take the stripes off a zebra's back.
As the sun sets,
The zebras have a rest.
After one last leap
The lion goes home and gets some sleep.

Havana Griffiths (6)
St John's CE Primary School & Nursery School, Swindon

My Max

My name is Max and I'm a dog,
I'm fluffy and brown and not a frog.
I chew my bones, run and play,
I bark and wag my tail all day.
When hometime comes and I am fed
I'm soon curled up asleep in bed.

Georgia Rose Salter (6)
St John's CE Primary School & Nursery School, Swindon

The Tale Of The Poor Flamingo

F lamingos put their heads in the water
L ong legs
A flamingo is pink
M y favourite bird
I t lives in the zoo
N ice big wings
G reat at standing on one leg
O nly eats fish.

Dhian Singh Sandhu (6)
Willington Primary School, Willington

The Hungry Elephant

E veryone loves them
L ive in Africa and the zoo
E at only plants
P eople can ride on them
H uge ears
A mazing tummy
N ot really fast
T runks for having a shower.

Paige Randle (6)
Willington Primary School, Willington

Sandy Rabbit

R eally nice carrots
A lot of white and brown fur
B ounce over the blue house
B ig flappy ears
I n a hutch she hops over hay
T ail is fluffy.

Lola Phillips (6)
Willington Primary School, Willington

Birds

B ig birds like food
I feed my bird at Granny's house
R eally high in the sky
D oes my bird love me? Yes he does
S tarlings and sparrows.

Olivia Stilwell (6)
Willington Primary School, Willington

My Dog Maddy

Doesn't like being on her own. She's happy to see us.
On a walk to Kadampa.
Gives her chicken and rice for tea.
Sleeps a lot in her bed.

Jack O'Connell (6)
Willington Primary School, Willington

Myrtle The Turtle

T wo eyes and four fins
U ntil they hatch
R eally slow
T hey have a hard shell
L ove to swim in the sea
E ats plants.

Mia Isabelle Fennell (6)
Willington Primary School, Willington

Gizmo The Dog

D og food is their favourite
O nly happy when someone is with them
G o to fetch the ball
S it on the bed for a nap.

Lacey Harrison (6)
Willington Primary School, Willington

Shark

S harp teeth to eat you
H ome is under water
A lways look for fish
R ace each other
K ill their dinner.

Hashim Ahmed (5)
Willington Primary School, Willington

Beautiful Bird

B irds have wings
I n the sky flying high
R ace in the sky in the fresh air
D ig the worms from the ground.

Harry Cooke (6)
Willington Primary School, Willington

Cats

C ats have soft fur
A ll the time cats miaow
T wo eyes, four legs, one tail
S troke my cat and it purrs.

Eli Jacob Cooling (6)
Willington Primary School, Willington

Duck

D ive under the water
U nhappy he's lost his friends
C atch bread in the pond
K ind to other ducks.

Jacob Bull (6)
Willington Primary School, Willington

Tigers

T hey are stripy
I n the jungle
G ood at catching stuff
E at meat
R eally sharp teeth.

Alba Grace Seals (6)
Willington Primary School, Willington

Lions

L ions have lovely fur
I n their mouth they have sharp teeth
O nly eat meat
N ever stroke them.

Vivienne Gough (6)
Willington Primary School, Willington

Rosie Lion

L ions have lovely fur
I t hunts for food
O n their paws are sharp claws
N ever get too close.

Lily Banks (6)
Willington Primary School, Willington

Fish

F ins help them in the water
I n the water racing around
S wim in the water
H ate each other.

Leon Zac Bryan (5)
Willington Primary School, Willington

Jemma The Lion

L ovely soft fur
I n the zoo they live
O utdoors they run around
N aughty little cubs.

Daisy Broadhurst (6)
Willington Primary School, Willington

Bird

B irds fly
I n the tree they build nests
R ace in the sky
D ive down to catch worms.

Maxwell Gene Arnold (6)
Willington Primary School, Willington

Fish

F inding more fish food
I love my fish
S wims in the tank
H as fins and a tail.

Lewis Richard Record (6)
Willington Primary School, Willington

Dog

D ark brown fur and tail
O utdoor play fighting together
G ive me the ball please!

Harley Neal (6)
Willington Primary School, Willington

Lily Cat

C atching tiny mice
A lways sleeping in their bed
T hey run around in the garden.

Ava Marsden (5)
Willington Primary School, Willington

Jack The Dog

D ogs like to lick you
O n a walk to the park
G ood at catching the ball.

Toby Sharp (6)
Willington Primary School, Willington

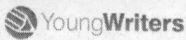

Jumping Frog

F rogs jump
R ound eyes
O nly eat insects
G reen skin.

Sienna Sahota (5)
Willington Primary School, Willington

Rose The Cat

C ats like to curl up
A lways purring
T hey like to scratch.

Eliza Bethany Scott (6)
Willington Primary School, Willington

Crazy Ape

A re good at climbing
P lay with friends
E at bananas.

Jayden Thomas (5)
Willington Primary School, Willington

Untitled

I have black and white feathers
Along with orange skin.
I achieve my full adult plumage
That is beautiful at around five years old.
I'm the smallest, old world vulture.
I eat eggs and carrion (meat)
So I'm a carnivore.
I can also be called a pharaoh's chicken.
I fly extremely quickly.
I live in pairs, normally in the middle
Of Africa, Europe and Asia
In the open country.
What am I?

Ryan Hailstone (7)
Worlaby Academy, Worlaby

Untitled

I am fierce and fearless
Because I scare humans and other animals.
I am powerful with soft brown and orange fur.
I have four strong legs.
I usually hunt at night but behave cleverly
Because I make traps to catch my prey.
I am a carnivore because I eat meat.
I am the only cat in groups called a pride.
I live in the dry grasslands of Africa.
What am I?

Taya Louise Williams (7)
Worlaby Academy, Worlaby

Untitled

I have a long grey trunk
And sharp white tusks.
My skin is dark, dull grey
But I am beautiful.
I am very powerful
Because I can pull up plants to eat.
I am the largest mammal on the land.
I am the largest animal in the land.
I have a baby called a calf.
I live in the dry grasslands of Africa.
What am I?

Rosie Harriss (6)
Worlaby Academy, Worlaby

What Am I?

I have a powerful, long, bumpy green tail.
I have four short legs.
I move slowly so that people don't see me.
I have sharp white teeth in my mouth to eat.
But I can survive without food for months.
I am a reptile.
I live in Africa but I also can be in zoos.
I also live under water.
What am I?

Tilly Rose Scott (7)
Worlaby Academy, Worlaby

What Am I?

I have bumps on my skin
And I am green.
I have four short legs
And I survive in water and on land.
I have a tail and I eat people and fish.
I am a reptile and I am fierce.
I am a fierce animal
And I live in Africa.
I am really slow and I live in water.
What am I?

Joey Roberts (6)
Worlaby Academy, Worlaby

Untitled

I am a fierce animal
And I have bright fur.
I have four strong legs
And sharp claws.
I am a carnivore.
I live in a group known as a pride.
I hunt for my prey at night.
I live in the dry grasslands of Africa.
What am I?

Ellie Hibbert (6)
Worlaby Academy, Worlaby

Untitled

I have dry, grey, wrinkly skin.
I have sharp white tusks.
I live in Africa
And I live on the dry grasslands.
I am the largest land mammal
But I am a herbivore.
My baby is called a calf.
What am I?

Freya Allen (6)
Worlaby Academy, Worlaby

Untitled

I have brown fur.
I am mean, cruel
And I am nasty.
I am a carnivore
And hunt my prey in the morning.
I live in a pride
And I eat animals.
I live in the grasslands of Africa.
What am I?

William George Fowler (6)
Worlaby Academy, Worlaby

Untitled

I have black and white stripes.
I look like a horse.
I have a black mane.
I eat leaves that means I'm a herbivore.
I live in the African grasslands.
I can run very fast.
What am I?

Alexandra Jorja Carter (6)
Worlaby Academy, Worlaby

African Poem

I have a furry mane.
I have four strong legs with sharp teeth
And claws.
I am a carnivore
And I hunt for my prey at night.
I live with my pride in Africa.
Who am I?

Lauren-Ava Brunyee (6)
Worlaby Academy, Worlaby

Untitled

I have black and white stripes.
I look like a horse.
I have a black mane.
I live in the African grasslands.
I eat grass and plants.
I run very fast.
What am I?

Edie Oliver (6)
Worlaby Academy, Worlaby

Untitled

I have black and yellow fur.
I have sharp teeth and claws.
I hunt for my prey.
I am a carnivore.
I live in Africa.
What am I?

Sophie Gravett (6)
Worlaby Academy, Worlaby

Untitled

I have sharp teeth.
I have bumpy skin.
I have claws.
I eat meat.
What am I?

Owen Phillips (6)
Worlaby Academy, Worlaby

What Am I?

I have a tail.
I am brown
And I am furry.
I eat meat.
What am I?

Theo Fletcher (5)
Worlaby Academy, Worlaby

Young Writers Information

We hope you have enjoyed reading this book – and that you will continue to in the coming years.

If you're a young writer who enjoys reading and creative writing, or the parent of an enthusiastic poet or story writer, do visit our website www.youngwriters.co.uk. Here you will find free competitions, workshops and games, as well as recommended reads, a poetry glossary and our blog.

If you would like to order further copies of this book, or any of our other titles give us a call or visit www.youngwriters.co.uk.

Young Writers, Remus House, Coltsfoot Drive, Peterborough, PE2 9BF
(01733) 890066

info@youngwriters.co.uk